A 12 WEEK STUDY

FOLLOWING
CHRIST

DISCOVERING THE UNLIMITED POWER AND JOY OF KNOWING CHRIST INTIMATELY

"My sheep listen to my voice; I know them, and they follow me."
John 10:27

STEVEN K SCOTT AND
MICHAEL SMALLEY, PH.D.

Published by Knowing Him
© 2016 Steven K. Scott

Knowing Him
26205 Oak Ridge Drive, Suite 119
The Woodlands TX 77380

ISBN

To order additional copies of this resource, visit www.knowinghim.com

Printed in the United States of America

To Our Kids

May you seek to love Jesus and desire above all else to do what He says.

About The Authors

....

Steven K. Scott

He is the New York Times best-selling author of numerous books, including The Greatest Words Ever Spoken, The Jesus Mission, and The Riches Man Who Ever Lived. Using the laws of success he learned from the book of Proverbs, Scott and his partners have built more than a dozen highly successful US and international companies. In his teaching ministry, Scott emphasizes the unique role and miraculous power of Jesus' words in the lives of believers. He says, "As we abide in Jesus' words, we can experience His fullness and come to know Him more intimately than we have ever imagined."

Michael Smalley, Ph.D.

Michael specializes in teaching people the principles of how to live out Jesus' greatest commands to love God and love others. His popularity as a renowned marriage and relationship expert quickly grew through his humorous stories and straightforward, no-nonsense advice. Michael's message inspires, motivates and challenges people to build better relationships.

His love story with his wife Amy began while he was an undergraduate at Baylor University. After graduation, Michael went on to earn a master's degree in clinical psychology from Wheaton College outside Chicago, Illinois and finished his Ph.D. at Barnham Theological Seminar in Houston, Texas.

Michael is the President of Knowing Him and also a co-founder, along with his wife Amy, of Smalley Institute and its premiere program for couples in crisis, the Reignite Marriage Intensive program. Traditional marriage counseling can be lengthy and frustrating and often couples can't find the time to make a positive impact on their relationships. Currently, the Smalley Institute has eight locations across the United States and even one in South Africa!

He has enjoyed over 22 years of marriage and makes his home in Magnolia, Texas. Michael has three children, Cole, Reagan, and David.

Table of Contents

Following Christ
Discovering the unlimited power and joy of knowing Christ intimately.
"My sheep listen to my voice; I know them, and they follow me." John 10:27

....

The heart of *Knowing Him* is to provide believers with an accelerated means of coming to know Jesus Christ more intimately, follow Him more fully, and lead others into that same kind of intimate relationship with Christ. Jesus said, "My sheep hear My voice, I know them and they follow Me. (John 10:27)

Our hope is you experience Jesus in a new way through the power of a small group. Meetings focused exclusively on the life and teachings of Jesus will give you a new passion to serve and follow Him like never before. Jesus said, "And this is eternal life, that they might know You, the only true God, and Jesus Christ whom you have sent." (John 17:3). By coming to know Christ more intimately, you also come to know the Father more intimately. In the Knowing Him small group format, you can take the commands and teachings of Christ, from the pages of your Bible, into the daily application and transformation of your life.

Knowing Him group meetings are not Bible studies, and **do not require leaders** who are skilled Bible teachers. They have a simple format in which the entire group facilitates the study time by simply following the discussion items. No skills are necessary to attend or host a meeting. The only requirement is that the people attending desire to get to know the Lord Jesus Christ more intimately. *Knowing Him* groups are designed to multiply. Anyone who attends a small group will be fully equipped to branch off and host a group of their own within six months of attending.

The meeting model

A Knowing Him group may consist of any small group, ranging from two people to twenty. It can be a men's or women's group, a mixed group, adults or youth. It can meet once a week, once every two weeks or even once a month. (Once a week or once every two weeks is what we would suggest.)

Beginning
Like most small group meetings, the Knowing Him meeting begins with fellowship, sharing and prayer. You can use this time to meet and share personal application of the teaching of Christ that was studied at the previous week's meeting. It is an opportunity to keep each other accountable to the action steps talked about from the previous week's study.

Study Time

Just follow these few simple steps as you begin the study time:

1. Play the lesson video for the particular week you are on. Each video gives you an overview of what you are studying.
2. Go over the lesson content next, this can be read before the group meeting or during the group (depending on what the group prefers).
3. The most powerful part is next, as a group go through the discussion section titled, "Following Jesus - What is He saying to me?". This is a valuable time for everyone to participate in understanding Jesus' words and applying them to their lives.
4. For further insight and study, each lesson has a reference to the book, *The Greatest Words Ever Spoken*. We provide you with the topic and page reference you can turn to in the book to dig deeper on the lesson's focus. You do not have to have, *The Greatest Words Ever Spoken*, in order to complete this study. It is only meant to provide extra insight for those who want to study the topic further.

Closing

When the group is done discussing the lesson, you can close with a simple prayer. If your group gets really involved with the discussion time, do not hesitate to pick it back during the next week to finish any discussion.

The unique role and power of Jesus words

. . . .

The Greatest Words Ever Spoken, Pages 62-64

The 20 Promises Jesus Made About His Words

Amazingly, Jesus made 20 promises to believers about the words He spoke that He did not make about any other words recorded in Scripture. This does not mean that his promises do not apply to the rest of the Word of God, but it does mean that He definitively made them about His words. For example, in John 6:63, Jesus said, "My words are spirit and life." His words are not simply "informational" in nature, but rather they literally infuse spirit and life into the hearts of those who embrace them, and they empower those who pattern their choices and behavior according to their instruction. Whenever we feel spiritually drained or inadequate, or feel depressed or even lifeless, chances are very high that we are not spending time focusing upon the words and teachings of Jesus.

In John 8:31-32, He made three life-changing promises to His followers who would "abide" in His word. He said, "If you abide in my word, then you are truly my disciples. And you shall know the truth, and the truth shall set you free." Here there are three promises that require one condition to be fulfilled on our part. The condition is that we must "abide" in His word. The word "abide," means to stop and dwell at a particular place. Abiding in Jesus' words means living in the midst of those words. Figuratively, it means eating, drinking and breathing them into the very fabric of who you are. It means taking them so seriously that you incorporate them into your daily choices and behavior. When we do this, He promises that we will become his "true" disciples, that we will KNOW the truth, and that the truth will set us free from being a slave to our sin nature.

As you read the topic, "The Role and Power of Jesus Words," (pages 62-64) underline the promises that He makes to those who abide in his words, and obey His teachings and commands. Here are the promises he makes, see if you can find the verses where He makes them. **Remember, you can find these on pages 62-64 in The Greatest Words Ever Spoken.**

_____ You will become His true Disciple

_____ You will receive knowledge of the Truth

_____ You will be Liberated from enslavement to sin

_____ You will gain Intimacy with Son and Father

_____ You will be Loved by the Father and Son in a special way

_____ He will disclose or reveal himself to you

_____ The Father and Son will come to you

_____ The Father and Son will make their home with you

_____ You will be cleansed from your sin

_____ Your Prayer requests will be answered

_____ You will bear much eternal fruit

_____ You'll dwell or REMAIN in His Love

_____ Jesus' joy will be in you

_____ Your joy will be full (complete, overflowing)

_____ Your "house" or life will not be destroyed

_____ Your life will be built on the perfect foundation

_____ You will be intimately "KNOWN" by Him

_____ You will have Assurance of your eternal life

_____ Your life and faith will not even be "shaken"

_____ You'll have ongoing infusion of Spirit and Life

Following Jesus — What is He Saying To Me?

During your week of meditating on Jesus' statements on the role and power of His words, use the lined pages that follow to record any thoughts, feelings or revelations that you have received during the week, as you receive them or later as time permits. The optional questions below are provided to help you journal your thoughts if you choose.

What Jesus has revealed to me about Himself and His words, teachings and commands?

_____

_____

_____

What Jesus has revealed to me about me? (For example, how should I be viewing His words in relation to me, my beliefs, and my choices and my behavior?)

_____

_____

_____

His will for me?

_____

_____

_____

His wisdom and Will for my relationship with Him?

_____

_____

_____

How can I apply what He is showing me to my relationship with my spouse?

_____

_____

_____

How can I apply what He is showing me to my relationship with my children and others?

_____

_____

Other insights and revelations that I've received and how can I apply them:

_____

_____

_____

Loving the Father and the Son

....

The Greatest Words Ever Spoken, Pages 110 and 280

In I John 4:18, the Apostle John tells us, "We love Him because He first loved us." When we are born again, the Holy Spirit enters into a union with our spirit, empowering us to experience and express the fruits of the Spirit. Agape love is the first fruit of the Spirit listed in Galatians 5:22. We are not only empowered to express agape love toward others, but toward God as well. Not only is He the source of this love, but Jesus' sacrifice on the cross is our greatest reason for loving Him. He died in our place, experiencing all of God's wrath and judgment for our sin.

In Luke 7:40-48, Jesus tells us that those who have a true realization of the hopelessness of their own sins and the magnitude of their incalculable debt to God, will be the ones who will experience and express the most love for God. As we discussed in the beginning of this journal, the greatest way we can express our love for God is to express it in the way that is most desirable to Him. As you meditate upon the statements of the Lord Jesus included in this topic, you'll begin to discover how you can love God in the very ways He wants to be loved.

Following Jesus—What is He Saying To Me?

During your week of meditating on Jesus' statements on "Loving God," use the lined pages that follow to record any thoughts, feelings or revelations that you have received during the week, as you receive them or later as time permits. The optional questions below are provided to help you journal your thoughts if you choose.

What Jesus has revealed to me about how I can love Him and God the Father?

_____

_____

_____

What Jesus has revealed to me about me and my love for Him? (For example, what can I do to love God more?)

_____

_____

_____

How can I love God when I don't "feel" anything?

_____

_____

_____

How is loving God different from loving people such as my spouse, children, parents, siblings or friends?

_____

_____

_____

What Jesus has revealed to me about His specific will this week.

His will for me?

_____

_____

_____

His wisdom and Will for my relationship with Him?

_____

_____

_____

Other insights and revelations that I've received and how can I apply them.

_____

_____

_____

Prayer - intimacy, answers, and power

···

The Greatest Words Ever Spoken, Pages 295-298

Prayer is like a diamond, in that it has a core or essence. and at the same time, many beautiful facets that break the light into a rainbow of sparkling colors. The core or essence of prayer is stated in Philippians 4:6-7. We are told, "Be anxious for nothing, but in everything by prayer and supplication, with thanksgiving, let your requests be made known to God; and the peace of God, which surpasses all understanding, will guard your hearts and minds through Christ Jesus." In other words, we shouldn't hold anything back, but tell the Lord our thoughts, wants, desires, and feelings, whatever they may be, in complete honesty and transparency. When we do, we aren't promised that we will receive what we have prayed for, but we will instead receive something else. By being totally honest with the Lord, even about our sinful desires, we are promised that He will give us peace--a type of "peace" that will go way beyond our own understanding. In fact, that peace is so powerful that it will actively keep watch and guard our hearts and minds through the person and power of Jesus Christ Himself. This is the type of prayer Paul was talking about when he said, "Pray without ceasing." (I Thes. 5:17) This type of prayer is not formal or structured—it doesn't require a special time or place or even faith. It is simply a way for us to express to God who we really are and what we really want.

However, just like that diamond, prayer has incredible facets that make it even more wonderful and valuable to our lives and the lives of those we interact with. For example, Jesus reveals the role and power of adding "faith" to our prayers, the power of fasting and praying, and what we can expect when we pray in His name. And that's only the beginning. He relates prayer to worship and praising the Father, seeking His will, gaining a forgiving heart toward those who offend us, and protecting us from temptation and Satan himself.

On pages 295-298 you'll find every statement that Jesus made on the subject of prayer. And on pages 53-55 you'll find the prayers that Jesus prayed that were recorded by the New Testament writers. All of His statements and prayers provide us with wisdom and insights on how we can have a far more effective prayer life. While the essence of prayer (Philippians 4:6-7) applies to any situation we will ever find ourselves in, some of the facets Jesus reveals may apply to some situations and not to others.

For example, asking for something, "in My name" applies to those situations where we know precisely what Jesus would ask for if He were physically present. Praying for something in His name does not simply mean closing a prayer or making a request, "in the name of Jesus." It literally means acting in His behalf, and according to two verses, acting in His behalf in a way that will bring "glory" to God and produce an abundance of spiritual fruit.

Following Jesus—What is He Saying To Me?

During your week of meditating on Jesus' statements on "Prayer," use the lined pages that follow to record any thoughts, feelings or revelations that you have received during the week, as you receive them or later as time permits. The optional questions below are provided to help you journal your thoughts if you choose.

In John 15:7-8, what are the two conditions Jesus gives for Him to give you whatever you ask? (Hint, the word that the NIV renders "remain" is translated "abide" in other New Testament translations). Also for what purposes will He give you what you ask for?

Make a list of the attributes that should be included in your prayers according to Matthew 6:9-13

_____   _____

_____   _____

_____   _____

What did Jesus say to you about praying in secret?

_____

_____

_____

What did Jesus say in Matthew 17:19-21 about coming against spiritual forces such as demons?

_____

_____

_____

What are the three activities we are instructed to do in Matthew 7:7-11

_____

_____

_____

What did Jesus say about praying with others in Matthew 18:18-20

_____

_____

_____

What other revelations and insights has Jesus revealed to you regarding prayer in general and your praying specifically?

_____

_____

_____

According to His teachings on prayer, where have you fallen short in your own prayer life in relation to what He has taught?

_____

_____

_____

What specific teachings can you now begin to incorporate into your prayer life more regularly?

_____

_____

_____

Faith - transforming and miraculous

. . . .

The Greatest Words Ever Spoken, Pages 445-451; 231-237

The Apostle Paul recorded a number of awesome revelations about "faith". He tells that we are "justified" by our faith in Christ. (Rom. 5:1) He tells us that faith is the means by which we embrace the very grace of God that saves us. (Eph. 2:8). He tells us that the Word of God actually produces faith within us. (Rom. 10:17) He says that without faith it is impossible to please God (Heb. 11:6), and that our faith in Christ produces a level of righteousness that can not be achieved by man, any other way. (Rom. 4:5, 13) He says faith is both our shield and the protector of our heart. (Eph. 6:16; I Thes.5-8) And in Hebrews 11:1, Paul said faith is so real that it is both a substance, and the evidence of spiritual realities that are in themselves, invisible. And finally, He tells us that Jesus is the author and perfecter of our faith. In other words, Jesus, who He is, what He did, and what He said actually produces faith within us and ultimately perfects that faith.

Faith Defined

Today, faith can be a very misunderstood concept. Some people equate it with positive thinking, others view it as mystical or a religious attitude. But it's true definition is much simpler than that. The Greek word for faith is pisteo. It literally means to totally rely upon. It means to totally entrust yourself. When you sit in a chair, you are expressing faith in that chair and its ability to support your weight. When you step into an airliner, you are expressing faith in that plane, the pilot and the airline company. The truth is, we are all creatures of faith. All of our actions are expressions of what we believe and what we believe in. But the only kind of faith that relates to our eternal destiny, and righteousness before God is our faith in the Father, Son and Holy Spirit. To express that faith means to listen to what God says, and the do it! In Hebrews 5:9, the Apostle tells us that Jesus is the "author of eternal salvation to all who obey Him." And in the Great Commission, Jesus tells his disciples, to make disciples of all nations, "teaching them to observe all things that I have commanded you."

So the essence of faith in Christ is to totally entrust yourself or rely upon Him and what He said as absolute truth. When we do that, the result is our behavior in any given situation reflects our true beliefs. So for faith to be present, we must first hear the word. Without hearing God's word for any given situation or moment, we cannot experience or express faith. That's why Paul said, "faith comes by hearing, and hearing by the word of God." If we diagramed it, it would look like this:

God---statement-----faith----behavior that is an expression of my faith in that statement.

Faith is not blind, nor without a word. Faith is not doing what you think Jesus would do. Faith in Christ is doing what He said for us to do in a given moment. When Peter saw Jesus walking on water, Peter wanted to do the same—but wanting to do it wasn't enough. Peter knew that He must first receive the word from Jesus. He said, "Lord, if it is You, command me to come to You on the water." (Matt. 14:29) The Jesus simply gave Him a single word, "come." And with that, Peter's faith was both created and expressed—and he became the only other man who walked on water.

The greatest source and opportunity for faith that we have, are the commands of Christ, (Greatest Words, 206-213) and the promises of Christ (Greatest Words, 298-304). Under those topics, Jesus gives over 130 commands and more than 100 conditional promises to his followers. There is virtually no situation we will ever encounter that He has not given us a word, a command, or a promise for---a word, a command or a promise that will produce in us faith and empower us to express that faith through our choices, actions and behavior. That's why Jesus revealed that the third ministry of the Holy Spirit is to bring to our "memory, whatsoever things I have said unto you." (John 14:26) But we deny the Holy Spirit that ministry in our life when we haven't even heard what the words Jesus said.

In your meditating upon Jesus' statements about faith and as you read the examples of how others demonstrated their faith in Him, you will see first hand the power and the "fruit" produced by faith in Christ and His words. On pages 445-451 of Greatest Words you'll find Jesus' statements about faith and belief in Him. In this section we have the very words that the Holy Spirit uses to produce in us His saving faith. On pages 231-237, we have examples of people who "heard" Jesus words and expressed and demonstrated their resulting faith. So in these two sections we receive instruction in faith from the very author and perfecter of our faith, and then we see living examples of the kind of behavior true faith produces.

Following Jesus—What is He Saying To Me?

During your week of meditating on Jesus' statements on "Faith," use the lined pages that follow to record any thoughts, feelings or revelations that you have received during the week, as you receive them or later as time permits. The optional questions below are provided to help you journal your thoughts if you choose.

Greatest Words, Pages 445-451

In John 5:24, Jesus reveal two thing that must happen for a person to have eternal life—what are they?

_____

_____

In John 6:29, what does Jesus reveal to be, "the work of God" and what does that mean to you?

_____

_____

_____

What can we expect to see in our life when we truly "believe" in Christ? (John 7:38)

_____

_____

_____

What other insights and revelations have you received while meditating upon Jesus words in this topic?

_____

_____

_____

Greatest Words, Pages 231-237

Write down the insights and revelations you see in the various examples of faith given in these pages.

_____

_____

_____

Write down situations where you could have expressed faith by acting upon His words, but you did not.

_____

_____

_____

Write down situations you are now facing where you need knowledge of His words to act in faith, and describe what action you think faith would produce in those situations.

_____

_____

_____

Missions of a Christian

....

The Greatest Words Ever Spoken, Pages 281-289

God is not a God of Chaos, Coincidence or "Go with the Flow." God is a God of purpose and destiny. He is truly the ultimate sovereign. In Matthew 25:14-30, Jesus teaches the parable of the talents. Before leaving for a long journey, The Master divides his wealth among three money managers, giving each one an appropriate amount to manage, according to their own ability. When he returned from his journey he found that two had diligently worked and managed his money, doubling what he had entrusted to them. The third had buried what had been entrusted to him, making no profit or return on the investment whatsoever. The two that had been diligent were praised and rewarded. The other one was not only called lazy, he was called wicked. For the entire duration of the master's trip, this man had received wages and room and board. And yet he neither pursued nor accomplished the mission the master had given him. Instead of praise or promotion, he was harshly criticized, fired and thrown out of the master's home.

Today, our natural tendency when it comes to "following Christ," is to just, "go with the flow". If we had an unlimited amount of time, and our Master had no purpose for us and no missions to entrust to us, that kind of serving might be okay. But we do have a limited amount of time, He does have a purpose for us and He has revealed specific missions that He wants us to diligently pursue and accomplish during our lifetime. He doesn't want us to just be purpose or mission driven… He wants us to be mission accomplished! Our missions, like any mission, include "do's" and "don'ts" which will help us to accomplish each mission in less time, and ultimately enable us to "bear much fruit."

In this topic, Jesus' statements reveal a number of missions He wants us to focus on and various sets of instructions to follow. Jesus never wasted words—He meant every word He ever said and wants His followers Him to take His words seriously. His words are not only critical to the success of our missions, they can literally make an eternal difference in our lives and the lives of those who cross our paths and our descendants for generations to come.

One American soldier took Jesus' instructions seriously. As he and his division were liberating Romania from the Nazi's, He shared the Gospel with a a Rumanian young man that he met. That young man became a Christian, and his conversion powered the underground church in Romania throughout the 44 years of communist rule that lasted until 1989. And as soon as the communist regime collapsed, it was this man's children and grandchildren that evangelized Rumania, and are now responsible for evangelizing all 12,000 towns and villages throughout Rumania! All because one American Soldier took his mission assignment from His Savior as seriously as he took his military assignments from his military commander.

Please don't insult God by minimizing your value to His kingdom. Remember the worth of one soul…that all of Heaven rejoices when one sinner repents!

Following Jesus—What is He Saying To Me?

During your week of meditating on Jesus' statements on "Missions of Christians," use the lined pages that follow to record any thoughts, feelings or revelations that you have received during the week, as you receive them or later as time permits. The optional questions below are provided to help you journal your thoughts if you choose.

Greatest Words, Pages 281-289

Below are a number of the Missions Jesus wants us to focus on during our lifetime. Write the verse reference in the blank space next to each mission.
In your journaling, write down what some of these missions mean to you, and how you can apply them to your life right now and situations you are going through.

Missions and Mission instructions for Christians

1. Open your eyes, look at the fields.
2. Begin sowing and reaping
3. Remain (abide) in Christ
4. Bear much fruit
5. Love each other as He loves us
6. Do what Jesus commands
7. Be sanctified
8. Become "unified" in Him.
9. Feed his lambs
10. Take care of his sheep
11. Follow Jesus
12. Become "fishermen of men"
13. Be the Salt of the Earth
14. Be the Light of the World
15. Let your light shine before men (let them see your good deeds & praise God)
16. Practice and Teach Jesus' commands
17. Become mature, and complete
18. Don't store treasures for yourself on earth
19. Store up treasures in heaven for yourselves
20. Serve God, not money
21. Don't worry about your life, your clothes, food, shelter, needs.
22. Seek FIRST his kingdom and his righteousness
23. Don't worry about tomorrow or future
24. Proclaim in the day, what He whispers in your ear.
25. Don't be afraid of those who kill the body
26. Fear God

27. Acknowledge Jesus before men
28. Love Jesus more than Mother or Father, Son or Daughter (his type of love)
29. Lose your life for my sake
30. Take his yoke upon you
31. Learn from Jesus
32. Make disciples of all nations& and Baptize them.
33. Teach them to OBEY all that He has commanded us.
34. Go into all world, preach Gospel to all creation
35. Worship the Lord and serve Him alone
36. Don't be afraid
37. Catch men
38. Hear his words and put them into practice
39. Don't look back-don't live in past
40. Ask the lord to send forth workers
41. Go out as lambs
42. Be on your guard against the arrogance and hypocrisy of pharisees.
43. Do not set your heart upon food, drink or clothes
44. Be dressed, ready for service
45. Do what he commands until he returns
46. Have grateful spirit not entitlement spirit
47. Give to gov't and others what is there due, and give to God what is his.
48. Strengthen your brothers and sisters
49. Preach repentance and forgiveness of sins in His name
50. Be his witnesses,
51. Overcome the distractions and temptations of the world
52. Don't be afraid of what you're about to suffer.
53. Be faithful to the point of death
54. Wake up
55. Endure patiently
56. Focus on purity, righteousness, virtue and what you put in front of your eyes.

Which of these missions of a Christian stand out most to you?

Mission #_____   Why?

_____

_____

_____

Mission #_____   Why?

_____

_____

_____

Mission #_____   Why?

_____

_____

_____

What Jesus said about anxiety, worry, and fear

....

The Greatest Words Ever Spoken, Pages 190-193

We've all experienced varying degrees of anxiety, worry and fear. Nearly always these feelings arrive when we anticipate or experience situations over which we have little to no control. Often times, the less control we have, the greater the anxiety. And if the situation is potentially life altering (such as a job loss, a divorce, a chronic illness or potential death, the anxiety level rises to the level of fear. For unbelievers, there's no solace or hope I can give that can help them overcome their anxiety or fear. But for those who are followers of Christ, I can tell you with certainty, He can absolutely free you from even the greatest worries and concerns and empower you to overcome any fear that will ever crowd into your lives. It's not that He delivers you from all anxiety, worry and fear at one moment, once and for all, but rather, He can deliver you moment-by- moment, day-by-day.

As you'll see as you meditate upon His statements in this section, anxiety, worry and fear are simply thermometers—they don't create the problem, they simply reveal the problem. We tend to think that it is the adverse situation that is the problem…creating the worry or fear. But that's not really the case. According to Jesus, our real problem is unbelief. Every time His disciples became anxious or afraid, he pointed out that their real problem wasn't their adversity, it was the fact that they lacked faith—they weren't entrusting their situation, future or destiny to Him. He had demonstrated that He was worthy of their faith. They had witnessed his miracles first hand. He had even commanded them to believe and trust in Him. And yet, time after time, they disobeyed His commands, ignored his words, and chose to fear rather than believe. We are no different. More often than not, we chose to focus on our adversity rather than on His words. When we are first confronted by an adverse situation, our natural immediate reaction is to worry and become afraid. But after that initial response, we have a choice—to remain anxious and afraid, or to discover or recall what Jesus said and exercise faith and trust in Him and His words. If we choose to remain in fear, we are being disobedient to His word. That's why the Apostle Paul said, "whatsoever is not of faith, is sin." (Rom. 10:14)

Does this mean that "feeling" afraid is sin? Absolutely not! For our emotions are not a function of our will… but our behavior is. Faith chooses to do what we are commanded to do in any situation, regardless of our feelings. When we chose to act in faith, our feelings of fear will soon be transformed into feelings of peace and confidence.

On May 26, 2008, I received a message that one of my sons had been diagnosed with cancer and was returning to the United States for emergency surgery and cancer treatment. My publisher had sent me a pre-release copy of Greatest Words. I instantly turned to page 190 and began to read Jesus' statements on the topic of anxiety, worry and fear. Within minutes, He had given me a number of specific changes He wanted in my behavior—as His follower, and as a husband and father. Equally important I began to receive a miraculous peace—not a complete deliverance from my fears, but a deliverance from the incapacitating feelings of fear that had been controlling my thoughts and behavior.

That night, a pastor that I had only known for 3 days, prayed for my son, asking that the tumor would be vaporized and that the surgeon would say four things on the day of surgery that would be a testimony of God's miraculous healing. After he prayed, he told me, "God answered my prayer, your son is fine, you have absolutely nothing to worry about." Although I believed that God was in control and that my son would receive His perfect will, I did not believe that the tumor was gone and that the doctor would say the four things that the pastor had prayed he would say. One week later, my son was operated on at our university hospital. The doctor literally called us from the operating room and said the three of the four phrases verbatim. He said, "I'm confused," "I couldn't find the cancer," and, "I don't understand this." The large tumor that had been photographed 7 days earlier, (a number of ultra-sounds from different angles) was gone. When He came out to see us an hour later, his first statement to us was the fourth phrase verbatim—"I have NEVER seen ANYTHING like this!" When I called the pastor the next day, and told him that the tumor was gone and the surgeon had said all four phrases verbatim, he said, "I know…I told you that night that God had answered our prayer."

Does this mean it's always God's will to heal and whether or not He does is simply a matter of our faith or lack of it? Absolutely not!!!. But this time, in this circumstance, it was His will and I am so grateful that it was. Equally, I am so glad that He brought a man into my path to boldly pray with faith. But God would have been a God of no less mercy, grace and glory had his will been to take my son to Heaven—He would have just had a different purpose!

However, as I read His statements regarding anxiety, worry and fear, had I continued to behave in fear, rather than trusting in Him and His words, then I would have been choosing to sin---for acting in fear in light of His commands not to, is disobeying the very God who redeemed me with His blood.

As you read Jesus statements on pages 190-193, you'll see such commands as "Don't be afraid" and "just believe," and "stop doubting," numerous times. You'll hear Him say, "trust in God, trust also in me." Oh what a blessed Savior we have. And in the times we live in, His words on this topic will be some of the most important words we will ever read.

Following Jesus—What is He Saying To Me?

During your week of meditating on Jesus' statements on "Anxiety, Worry and Fear" use the lined pages that follow to record any thoughts, feelings or revelations that you have received during the week, as you receive them or later as time permits. The optional questions below are provided to help you journal your thoughts if you choose.

Greatest Words, Pages 190-193

In John 6:20 Jesus tells his terrified disciples, "It is I; Don't be afraid." And in John 14:1, Jesus said to those same disciples, "Do not let your hearts be troubled. Trust in God; trust also in me. In these statements He reveals:

That He is the reason to not be afraid, and that whether or not our hearts are troubled, is not a function of our circumstances, but is solely a function of our choice.

And the choice He offers that will liberate our hearts from being troubled is choosing to trust in the Father and in Him.

To be afraid or let our hearts be troubled is to choose to disobey His command and remain in unbelief.

We also discover that fear comes from our hearts not just our minds—and reveals unbelief in our hearts.

But as His words pass through minds and are driven into our hearts by the ministry of the Holy Spirit, our hearts can be transformed from unbelief to faith.

All of this is just from two passages. Write out the insights and revelations you receive as you read the other 22 passages under this topic.

Write some of the adversity you are currently experiencing and the worries or fears you are going through.

_____

_____

_____

How can you apply the revelations you receive from these passages and Jesus' commands to believe, trust, and stop doubting, to the worries and fears you are currently experiencing?

_____

_____

_____

God's love, grace, and mercy

∙∙

The Greatest Words Ever Spoken, Pages 99-102, 424-427

As a young Christian in college, I attended Scottsdale Bible Church and sat under the gifted Bible teaching and preaching of Dr. James Borror. One Sunday, he started his sermon with a simple question—"If God eliminated all evil from the planet at 12:00 midnight…where would you be at 12:01?" Certainly, the most amazing miracle ever performed is the spiritual miracle of cleansing the human soul from all of its sin---and trading that sin and all of its consequences on the sacrificial Lamb of God, and at the same time transferring all of His righteousness to our human soul. (II Corinthians 5:21)

Paul tells us in Ephesians that we were "dead in sin," and "having no hope." Both of those statements are absolutes. There are no degrees of "dead." Dead means no life or chance of future life whatsoever. "No hope," doesn't mean almost none—it means NO hope… WHATSOEVER! And then there's the best news ever published. In Ephesians 2:4-7, we find one of the most glorious statements in all of scripture—a statement that starts with the two words that change everything…"BUT GOD!" "But God, who is rich in mercy, because of His great love with which He has loved us, even when we were dead in trespasses, made us alive together with Christ (by grace you have been saved), and raised us up together, and made us sit together in the heavenly places in Christ Jesus, that in the ages to come He might show the exceeding riches of His grace in His kindness toward us in Christ Jesus."

All that we have of value, both now and for eternity, has come to us because of God's love, grace and mercy. When criticized by the religious leaders for associating with sinners, Jesus said, "Those who are well have no need of a physician, but those who are sick. But go and learn what this means: 'I desire mercy and not sacrifice.'" (Matthew 9:13 NKJV) Yes, God is perfectly Holy, Righteous and Just. But thankfully for us, He is also "rich" in mercy, grace and love. And nowhere is God's love and grace more apparent or more audibly heard or visibly seen, then in the Lord Jesus Christ, His life and His words.

Following Jesus—What is He Saying To Me?

During your week of meditating on Jesus' statements on "God's Love, Grace and Mercy," use the lined pages that follow to record any thoughts, feelings or revelations that you have received during the week, as you receive them or later as time permits. The optional questions below are provided to help you journal your thoughts if you choose.

Greatest Words, Pages 99-102, 424-427

In John 3:14, Jesus foretells His crucifixion with a reference to Moses lifting up the serpent and then reveals that it was the love of God the Father that sent Him to become the way through which believers could receive eternal life. In John 5:42, Jesus reveals that the Love of God can actually become a resident of the Human heart or soul. But he also revealed that those he was talking to did not have God's love in their hearts. On what basis did He make that judgment.

In John 14:21 and 14:23, Jesus tells of a very special kind of love that He and the Father will demonstrate uniquely to people who do something in particular. What did He call upon these people to do to receive this special love from God? How will the Father and the Son show this special love to these people?

_____

_____

_____

How did the God demonstrate his mercy upon the man Jesus addressed in Mark 5:19

_____

_____

_____

In Luke 15: 11-32 Jesus gives the parable of the prodigal son. What does He reveal to you as you meditate upon this parable?

_____

_____

_____

In Matthew 6:26-33, what does Jesus say should be the outcome of God's love and care in our lives—what does is he saying to you in this passage?

_____

_____

How will God respond to His children who ask, seek and find, according to Matthew 7:7-11

_____

_____

_____

In Matthew 20:1-16, Jesus gives a parable that illustrates that God is free to show any level of love or mercy to anyone he wants—and if He shows more mercy or grace to one than He does to the other, rather than focus on the more abundant grace He showed another, we are to be grateful for the grace he has shown to us, even if it appears to be less. He is free to do whatever He pleases, as we exist for His pleasure and purposes, not visa versa. Please meditate upon this passage prayerfully and write down any insights or revelations that apply to your life.

_____

_____

_____

Greatest Words, Pages 424-427

According to Luke 6:27-36, WHY are we to love our enemies, do good to people who hate us, bless those who curse us and pray for those who abuse or mistreat us? (Jesus tells us why toward the end of the passage.)

_____

_____

_____

What did the Lord tell Paul when Paul pleaded with the Lord to remove one of his trials? (II Corinthians 12:7-9). What situations at home or at work or in any area of your life could Jesus be saying the same thing to you?

_____

_____

_____

Forgiveness - the proof of our new birth

The Greatest Words Ever Spoken, Pages 142-143; 253-257; 481-483

In Matthew 6:14-15, Jesus said, "For if you forgive men when they sin against you, your heavenly Father will also forgive you. But if you do not forgive men their sins, your Father will not forgive your sins. "(NIV) In other words, a person who has been truly born again will be able to forgive those who sin against them. On the other hand, if you find it impossible to forgive someone, then you have good reason to question whether or not you have really been born again. How can this be? Jesus explains this in a parable in Matthew 18:23-35. Here he tells the parable of the servant who was forgiven a debt equal to billions of dollars, but then refused to forgive someone who owed him a debt equal to a few thousand dollars.

The analogy is clear. When his master found out that he had not shown the mercy to another when a much greater mercy had been shown to him, his debt was restored and he was sent to prison. Had he been truly transformed by the incredible mercy and forgiveness he had been shown, forgiving another of a lesser debt would have been a natural result of his transformation---but that transformation of his heart had never taken place. The person who is truly born again has been forgiven such an unfathomable and humanly unforgivable debt, that to not forgive someone else of a much lesser debt is proof that they have not been truly transformed by God's grace and mercy. They have not realized the hopelessness of their own sinful debt and amazing miracle of God's forgiveness of their sin and His gift of eternal life through the sacrifice of His own dear Son. They are still dead in sin.

But forgiveness is not only the proof of our salvation, it is the very currency with which we bless those who have wrongly offended us. Forgiveness from one's heart is something that cannot be counterfeited by our human nature or mere religion. It is a currency of our soul and it has only one source, God Himself. It is foreign to our human nature but it is a natural attribute of His nature—and a fruit of the Holy Spirit that indwells those who have been born again.

The word, "forgive" comes from the Greek word that means to untie and release. Forgiving someone is not a matter of having "feelings" of forgiveness, but rather choosing to release someone from the debt of their offense toward us, because God has released us from the debt of our sin toward Him. We forgive others as a means of loving God and obeying His will.

In The Greatest Words Ever Spoken, Jesus' teachings on forgiveness are divided into three sections: Forgiveness (253-57); Forgiveness of Sins (142-43); and Forgiveness of Others (481-83). I would suggest that you start with "Forgiveness of Sins," then read "Forgiveness," and conclude your meditation and study with "Forgiveness of Others." Some of the same passages are included in all three, but each topic has some verses that are only found under that topic.

Following Jesus—What is He Saying To Me?

During your week of meditating on Jesus' statements on "Forgiveness, Forgiveness of Sins and Forgiveness of Others, use the lined pages that follow to record any thoughts, feelings or revelations that you have received during the week, as you receive them or later as time permits. The optional questions below are provided to help you journal your thoughts if you choose.

Greatest Words, Pages 142-143; 253-257; 481-483 (142-143)

In Matthew 9:2, Jesus shocks His hearers when He tells a paralytic, "Your sins are forgiven." They all knew that God alone had the authority to forgive the sins of men on earth. But in Matthew 9:5-6, He proved that He shared that authority with God the Father. How did He prove it and what does that mean to you?

_____

_____

_____

In Matthew 26:28 Jesus reveals why His blood was shed—who was His blood shed for, and what did it accomplish?

_____

_____

_____

In Mark 11:25, if during your prayer time you remember that you haven't forgiven someone who has wronged you, what Does Jesus tell you to do at that moment.

_____

_____

_____

Why was the woman in Luke 7:44-48 able to love Jesus more than the others in the room?

_____

_____

_____

Greatest Words, Pages 253-57

According to John 3:14-21, what determines if a person is forgiven for their sins, or not forgiven?

_____

_____

_____

In John 8:7-12, who was the only one who was qualified to stone the woman caught in adultery? What Does He say to you about your sin in this passage and the path you should follow?

_____

_____

_____

What are His commands to you in Luke 6:37-38? Who are the people in your life that you have had a hard time forgiving? Who in your life have you been judgmental toward, and what should you do toward these people?

_____

_____

In Luke 17:3-6, Jesus gives some very hard instructions to his disciples and us regarding our forgiveness of others. What did he say? Why did His disciples instantly ask him to increase their faith?

_____

_____

_____

Why did Jesus send Paul to preach to the gentiles? (Acts 26:18)

_____

_____

_____

Greatest Words, Pages 481-483

Why must we forgive those who sin against us, regardless of their sin? (Matthew 6:14-15; Matthew 18:35)

_____

_____

_____

What other insights, revelations or commands do you see in Matthew 18:21-35?

_____

_____

_____

What is Jesus saying to you in all of this?

_____

_____

_____

How can you begin to apply His teachings on forgiveness to your specific relationships, right now?

_____

_____

_____

Love - infinite capacity, never ending flow

The Greatest Words Ever Spoken, Pages 278-280

One of the defining moments of my life was the day that Gary Smalley first told me that, "Love is not a feeling…It's a Decision". As a young man, I had felt inadequate in that I could not create feelings that simply did not exist. Since I thought love was a feeling, I felt my love toward God was woefully inadequate, and my love for most others also fell way short of what I believed God wanted me to feel. When Gary taught me that true love was a decision to act in loving ways, everything changed. Though I couldn't create feelings of love in my heart, I could express loving actions to anyone God placed in my path. I later discovered that every time Jesus talked about love, there was always a corresponding decision to do a loving action.

For example, in John 3:16, Jesus said, "For God so loved the world, that He gave His only begotten son." God's love has always been demonstrated with actions. And when it comes to loving Him, as we have already seen, Jesus defined love for Him and God the Father as simply doing what He says. In John 21:15-17, Jesus told Peter that he should express his love for Jesus by leading, guiding and feeding His "sheep." And in John chapters 13 and 15 Jesus issues and repeats a new commandment to His disciples (and to us), that we love one another in the same manner that He loves us! And when the Apostle Paul defined love in I Corinthians, he defined it with actions, not feelings.

Although Jesus didn't say a lot about love (only a handful of statements), what He said about it was both revolutionary and transformational. He not only told us to love our enemies, He told us how to do it—bless them and pray for them, and then demonstrated it on the cross when He interceded on their behalf when He prayed, "Father forgive them, for they know not what they do."

Our love for other believers is one of the marks of a true disciple of Christ. Our ability to love our enemies is a measure of our love for Him and our intimacy with Him. As Stephen was preaching to the men who hated him and had plotted his death he looked up toward heaven and saw Jesus standing at the right hand of God. And as his enemies were filled with hatred, they rushed him and stoned him to death. Yet his final words were, "Lord, do not charge them with this sin."

* It is important to note that the Sermon on the Mount and other teachings of Jesus on the subject of love, were meant to be followed at a personal level and were not teachings about governments and nations in their relations with each other.

Following Jesus—What is He Saying To Me?

During your week of meditating on Jesus' statements on "love" use the lined pages that follow to record any thoughts, feelings or revelations that you have received during the week, as you receive them or later as time permits. The optional questions below are provided to help you journal your thoughts if you choose.

Greatest Words, Pages 278-280

In Mark 12:31, Jesus tells us what He calls the second greatest commandment, "Love your neighbor as yourself." How can you specifically apply this command to:

Loving your spouse?

_____

_____

Loving your children?

_____

_____

Loving others who God brings into your path?

_____

_____

In Luke 6:27-36, shows us how we are to love our enemies—he tells us to love them, bless them and pray for them. And then he gives us specific examples of what that kind of love would look like.

_____

_____

_____

List people that you interact with that you don't "like" or even worse, "can't stand," and prayerfully ask the Lord what He would like you to do to begin to implement these very hard commands into your relationships with those people.

_____

_____

_____

- Note: loving our enemies does not mean entering into a co-dependent relationship or partnership with them. There are a lot of very evil people in our world—although Jesus wants us to take loving action toward our enemies, He does not want us to be unequally "yoked" to them. He wants us to be, "wise as serpents and harmless as doves," in all of our dealings with those who don't know and love Him (Matthew 10:16).

Resolving anger and conflict

....

Greatest Words Pages 474; 477-480;487-488

Anger is an emotion that every man, woman, boy and girl experiences. Gary Smalley points out that Anger is a secondary emotion. In other words it always has one of three root causes that are the primary emotions that cause anger. Anger results from unresolved hurt, unresolved fear, or unresolved frustration, or a combination of these emotions. But regardless of its cause, left unattended, anger is the number one destroyer of relationships and can inflict permanent damage to individuals that can only be healed by the miraculous grace of God. Jesus was the first person on planet earth to identify the true, hideous nature of anger—saying that it is categorized by God as a sin as serious as murder. When we excuse it, minimize it or refuse to deal with it, then we are taking a course of action contrary to God's values and instructions.

Since anger is a secondary emotion, it is like a thermometer that tells us we have a deeper problem—namely a hurt, fear or frustration that hasn't been dealt with. The GREAT news is that through our relationship with the Lord, all three are easily dealt with. As we discovered in His words regarding "anxiety worry and fear," any unresolved fear reveals a situation or an area of our life where we are not believing God's word and not trusting Him. Once discovered, we can commit that situation to Him, and He will relieve our fears with a peace that surpasses human comprehension, supply us the grace we need and give us an answer in keeping with His perfect will.

On the other hand, a hurt or frustration always has it's root in our failure to yield our rights to the Lord. Someone has failed to live up to our expectations, wants or needs that we feel we have a right to be met. In Philippians 2:5-8 Paul reveals that just as Jesus gave up all of His rights in Heaven to come to earth, live and die as a man and servant of God," we are to give up all of our rights to also become a bond-servant of God. Any time we have a emotional hurt or frustration that has been inflicted by someone else, that hurt or frustration reveals an area of our life where we have failed to surrender our perceived rights to God. This is what Jesus meant when He tells all who would follow Him, "Take up your cross and follow me." (Mt. 10:38; 16:34) One who carries a cross is dying to their own self centeredness and has no rights whatsoever—not to happiness, not to health, not to honor, not to love, not to wealth. The man or woman who is carrying a cross following Christ is surrendering their rights, knowing that the eternal value of following Christ is far greater than any temporary sacrifice of perceived rights.

And here's the best news of all—when you do not feel entitled to anything, people can no longer hurt you. And when you feel entitled to nothing, you will become grateful for anything and everything good that comes your way. Just as an entitlement mentality makes it impossible to love and be happy, giving up all "rights" makes gratefulness and happiness a moment-by-moment reality!

And when it comes to conflict, Jesus not only tells us to resolve it quickly, He shows us how to resolve it—by giving the other person even more than they ask for! Wow. If we all followed Christ, there would be no need for lawyers or lawsuits. Oh how wonderful Heaven will be!

Following Jesus—What is He Saying To Me?

During your week of meditating on Jesus' statements on "Resolving Anger and Conflict," use the lined pages that follow to record any thoughts, feelings or revelations that you have received during the week, as you receive them or later as time permits. The optional questions below are provided to help you journal your thoughts if you choose.

Greatest Words Pages 474; 477-480;487-488

In Matthew 5:21-24, what does Jesus say you should do when you realize that you are angry with someone or you have offended them or they have offended you?

_____

_____

_____

Who can you think of that you should go and be reconciled with?

_____

_____

_____

Many of our conflicts are created by wrongly assessing other people's motives, words or actions. What does Jesus tell us to do in John 7:24 and John 8:7

_____

_____

_____

Who have you wrongly judged in the past? (May be a fairly long list).

_____

_____

_____

How are we to love our spouse and children? (John 13:34)

_____

_____

_____

How doe Jesus tell you to resolve conflict in Matthew 5:23-25 and Matthew 5:38-41?

_____

_____

_____

What is the consequence of judging others? (Matthew 7:1-5)

_____

_____

_____

How are we to respond when someone sins against us? (Matthew 18:15-17)

_____

_____

_____

How many times should we forgive a person, and why should we always forgive them?
Matthew 18:21-35

_____

_____

_____

According to Luke 6:37-38 what are the consequences of judging versus the benefits of giving?

_____

_____

_____

The promises of Jesus

···

The Greatest Words Ever Spoken, Pages 298-304

The Apostle Paul wrote, "So then, faith comes by hearing, and hearing by the word of God." (Romans 10:17 NKJV). The only way to receive salvation is by faith, and the only way to receive faith is by hearing what God has said. But the word of God not only creates faith, it is used as a tool by the Holy Spirit to grow and increase our faith. Every believer would love to have "more faith", but the only way to increase your faith is to focus your mind, heart and behavior upon the word of God. Over and over again, we see Jesus give a word or a command to individuals, they act upon that word and their faith performs a miracle in their life—but it all starts with a word from the Lord.

In this topic, we have over 100 conditional promises that Jesus made to His followers. A conditional promise simply means that He will perform what ever His word says He'll perform, so long as you meet the condition included in the promise. For example John 14:21 says, "He who has My commandments and keeps them is the one who loves Me; and he who loves Me will be loved by My Father, and I will love him and disclose Myself to him."

In this one statement Jesus makes 3 promises to you, based upon you meeting one and only one condition. He promises that: (1) the Father will actively love you; (2) Jesus will actively love you; and (3) Jesus will disclose (reveal or manifest) Himself to you. Three amazing, unbelievable promises that He personally makes to you. The only condition is that you love Him the way He wants to be loved—namely, learn his teachings and commands, and practice them in your daily life. His promises are amazing, and their fulfillment in the life of believers is miraculous.

Following Jesus—What is He Saying To Me?

During your week of meditating on Jesus' statements on "Promises of Christ," use the lined pages that follow to record any thoughts, feelings or revelations that you have received during the week, as you receive them or later as time permits. The optional exercise below is provided to help you journal your thoughts if you choose.

The Greatest Words Ever Spoken, Pages 298-304

Below you will find 77 of the more than 100 conditional promises that Jesus makes to His followers. As you read through the verses in this topic, write the "condition" that needs to be met to receive the promised benefit, and write the verse reference in the appropriate blanks. These follow the order of the verses as they are presented under the topic. **You will find them in order starting on page 298 in The Greatest Words Ever Spoken.**

77 Conditional Promises to Jesus' Followers

	Promise	Condition	Verse
1	Eternal life		
2	Never die		
3	Avoid condemnation and judgment		
4	Has already crossed over from death to life		
5	Will come out of the grave		
6	Christ will never drive away or "cast out"		
7	Christ will raise up on last day		
8	Streams of living water will flow from within		
9	Will never walk in darkness		
10	Will have the LIGHT OF LIFE.		
11	Be his Disciples		
12	Shall know the truth		
13	Truth shall set you free from sin		
14	Will never SEE death		
15	Will be saved		
16	Will find pasture (fulfillment)		
17	Abundant life		
18	You will be Known by the Good Shepherd		
19	Can't be snatched out of Jesus hand		
20	Will LIVE (not just exist)		
21	Never die		
22	Won't remain in darkness		
23	Have a place prepared by Jesus, in heaven		
24	Jesus will come back for you		

	Promise	Condition	Verse
25	Jesus will take you with him to the place he has prepared		
26	Will do what He did, and Greater things		
27	He will do whatever you ask in His name.		
28	Will not leave you as an orphan		
29	We will live because he lives		
30	You will KNOW that He is in Father, the Father is in Him and He is in YOU.		
31	He will be IN you.		
32	Jesus will love you		
33	Jesus will show himself to you.		
34	You will be loved by the Father		
35	Jesus and Father will come to you and make their home with you		
36	Holy Spirit will teach you all things		
37	Holy Spirit will remind you of everything Jesus said to you.		
38	He will give you a "peace" that no one else and nothing else can.		
39	You will produce a lot of "eternal fruit"		
40	Ask whatever you wish, it will be given to you (in area of "bearing fruit")		
41	Remain in his love		
42	His joy will be in you, and your joy will be complete		
43	Your fruit will last.		
44	Holy Spirit will guide you in all truth		
45	Holy Spirit will testify of Christ		
46	Holy Spirit will tell you what's to come (future)		
47	Holy Spirit will take from Christ and reveal to you		
48	Peace in Christ.		

	Promise	Condition	Verse
49	Kingdom of Heaven		
50	Comfort		
51	Inherit the earth		
52	Filled with righteousness		
53	Obtain Mercy		
54	See God		
55	Called "Great" in the Kingdom of Heaven		
56	Reward from Father		
57	Forgiveness		
58	Everything you need		
59	What you Ask for, what you seek, and open doors		
60	Good gifts		
61	Endurance through storms of life and judgment		
62	Acknowledgment before God		
63	Blessings		
64	Rest		
65	Help		
66	Included in Family of God		
67	Whatever you bind on earth will be bound in heaven__		
68	What 2 or three ask for will be done by Father		
69	I will be in your midst		
70	100 times as much in this life and eternal life		
71	Whatever you ask for in prayer (matt 21:22)		
72	Inheritance prepared before the earth was created		
73	I will be with you till the very end		

	Promise	Condition	Verse
74	You won't be judged		
75	Given in great measure		
76	You'll become the greatest		
77	Given the Holy Spirit		

Spiritual priorities - achieving God's goals

The Greatest Words Ever Spoken, Pages 328-337

The Apostle James said, "For what is your life? It is even a vapor that appears for a little time and then vanishes away." (James 4:14, NKJV) Paul told us to, "redeem the time" (Colossians 4:5). Looking back at the Parable of the Talents, one lesson that shouldn't be missed, is that we all have an extremely limited amount of time on this earth. God wants us to "bear as much fruit" as He knows we are capable of bearing in the limited amount of time that we have. Jesus tells us that He is glorified when we do so. (John 15:8)

And yet, our lives are busier than ever, just trying to "get by." How can we bear the kind and the amount of "fruit" that God desires. We can't all just quit our jobs, or ignore the needs of our families and become foreign missionaries. Given the limited amount of time we have in our days, weeks and months, How can we achieve what God wants us to achieve. The answer isn't as complicated as you might think. He simply wants us to value what He values, and make His priorities our priorities.

For example, in Luke 16:15, Jesus said, to the super-religious Pharisees, "You are the ones who justify yourselves in the eyes of men, but God knows your hearts. What is highly valued among men is detestable in God's sight." Do you want to justify yourself, or be justified by God? Do you want to highly value what He detests, or do you want to value what He loves? Discovering His priorities not only allows us to bear much more eternal "fruit" in our limited amount of time, it enables us to discover what He loves and what He detests, so His values can become our values. But none of this happens naturally or automatically. Jesus said, "I am the light of the world. Whoever follows me will never walk in darkness, but will have the light of life." (John 8:12 NIV)

In the passages included in this topic, you will discover the spiritual priorities that Jesus identified for those who want to follow Him. Adopting his priorities as your priorities will empower you to "bear much fruit," and at the same time create a greater unity and deeper level of intimacy with the Lord Jesus.

Following Jesus—What is He Saying To Me?

During your week of meditating on Jesus' statements on "Spiritual Priorities" use the lined pages that follow to record any thoughts, feelings or revelations that you have received during the week, as you receive them or later as time permits.

The number of passages in this topic are more numerous than most topics, so you might want to spend two or three weeks meditating and journaling this topic. Because there are so many passages, we decided not to provide questions; but rather encourage you to meditate and journal without any prompting from us, and allow this to be a time of intimate prompting by the Holy Spirit.

Greatest Words, Pages 328-337

This is what God is teaching me:

_____

_____

_____

_____

_____

_____

_____

_____

_____

_____